All About Joshua Tree

The branches of the Joshua tree point every which way, inviting you to explore. But which way? To the low desert, where creosote bushes bake in the summer sun? Or to the high desert, home of the Joshua tree? Or to an oasis, where palm trees thrive?

Your choices are many, because two deserts meet in Joshua Tree National Park. The Mojave is higher, cooler, and a little wetter than the Colorado. These two different *ecosystems* are home to a surprising variety of plants and animals.

Protecting that *diversity* is the job of the National Park Service. It works to ensure that there will always be wild, open spaces—room for the Joshua trees to grow, their branches pointing toward discovery in every direction.

What do you mean by...? *If you find a word you don't understand, take a look on page 46. There's a list there that explains what some of the big words in this book mean.*

A is for **Arch Rock**.
Can you see an elephant's eye?
An elephant's mouth, an elephant's trunk,
Against an ele-phantastic sky?

A

B is for the **Bighorn Sheep**—
Their horns curl round and round.
Look for them high on cliffs,
On steep and rocky ground.

B

C is for the **Cactus Wren**
That nest among the yucca.
Calling chuh chuh chuh, chuh, chuh, chuh,
Do you think its song gets stuck-a?

C

Desert Drama

Deserts are hot, right? No, not necessarily. Deserts get cold. It even snows sometimes in the park. Deserts are deserts because they're dry. Deserts are places that receive less than ten inches of rain a year.

The drama of life in the desert is played on a stage of extremes: blazing hot summer days, freezing cold winter nights. At first glance, the stage might seem empty, almost lifeless. But a closer look reveals a diverse cast of plants and animals that have made the *adaptations* needed to survive.

A dead Joshua tree provides food, as well as a place to hide and rest, for animals from insects to lizards to birds.

Jackrabbits are cooled by blood circulating through their huge ears. Because plants can lose precious moisture through the surfaces of their leaves, cacti don't even have any! Every plant and animal must adapt to a harsh, dry environment to play its role in the desert drama.

D is for the **Desert**—
Winters freeze it, summers burn it.
But it's a place that's full of life
If you take the time to learn it.

D

E is for the **Eagle Mountains**
Reaching for the sky.
The scent of creosote fills the air,
And eagles soar on high.

E

F is for the **Kit Fox**—
Small hunter with great big ears
For cooling off from desert heat
While chasing the prey it hears.

Gold Fever

Gold fever is said to bring out the worst in people. That was the case with the McHaney brothers at the Desert Queen Mine. They were believed to have stolen gold from its owners by ambush. They worked the mine for years, made a fortune, then squandered their gains and lost their claim. One died poor, the other in jail. Their story is only one of many tales of gold, greed, boom, and bust from more than a century of mining in the park.

Mining changed the face of this place forever. The land is now riddled with holes and mine shafts. Many roads and trails were carved into this desert wilderness. Native plants and animals were displaced.

In 1936 new mining claims were outlawed at Joshua Tree. But the glitter of gold fever remains. Visit the old *stamp mill* at Lost Horse Mine or enjoy a shady rest at Cottonwood Springs, where a grove of trees was planted by *teamsters*, who hauled gold ore in horse-drawn wagons.

G is for the **Gold**
That brought miners to this land.
With pick and shovel, toil and sweat,
They dug the ore by hand.

H is for **Hidden Valley**,
Where cattle rustlers used to hide.
Now its towers and domes of rock
Are scaled by climbers from far and wide.

H

I is for **Indian Cove**,
Cozy amid the rocks.
One of the coolest places to camp,
Find a nook, hang up your socks!

I

The Joshua Tree: Wanted, Dead or Alive!

The Joshua tree is so cool, they named an entire national park after it. Alive, a Joshua tree offers birds a place to nest, and lots of insects to eat. Small seedling trees are a favorite food for deer, rabbits, and other animals.

Dead, the Joshua tree is still important to wildlife. Woodpeckers drill out nesting holes in the soft wood. A fallen tree becomes a hiding place for squirrels, scorpions, and wood rats. The rotting log is both home and food for termites, a favorite meal of the yucca night lizards that also live there.

The Joshua tree got its name from Mormon pioneers who passed through the California desert in the 1850s. They thought the trees looked like the biblical prophet Joshua, his hands raised in the air, praying for help to lead his people to the Promised Land.

J is for the **Joshua Tree**,
Branches pointing everywhere—
Like the ancient, bearded prophet
With his hands up in the air.

J

K is for the **Keys Ranch**—
It's also called the Desert Queen.
A chance to learn about the past
And see old buildings and machines.

K

Chuckwalla

Desert iguana

Collared lizard

L is for the **Lizards**.
The fringe-toed kind are rare,
But iguanas and chuckwallas
Can be seen most everywhere.

M is for the **Mojave Desert**,
Higher, wetter, and a little less hot.
Joshua trees are found in the Mojave—
In the low Colorado they're not.

N is for the **Night Sky**,
Sparkling with millions of stars.
You might see a comet, you might see the moon,
You might see a planet like Venus or Mars.

N

Oh So Delightful!

Green never looked so good! In a sea of desert browns, palm trees stand out like a postcard from another place and time... an *oasis* in the desert.

Five oases are scattered across the park. They are found where enough water seeps from the ground, or occurs just below the surface, to support plants not usually found in the desert.

Oases are magnets for both people and animals. Native American Indians, prospectors, and ranchers all sought out the park's oases for water and a bit of shade. Lush plant life and the chance for a drink attract lots of wildlife, especially birds.

Park headquarters and the Oasis Visitor Center are located next to the Oasis of Mara, which takes its name from an Indian word meaning "place of small springs and much grass."

O is for **Oasis**,
Where water seeps up from the ground.
Palm trees mark these places where
Plants and animals abound.

"...the strangeness and wonder of existence are emphasized here, in the desert...life not crowded upon life as in other places but scattered abroad in spareness and simplicity...."

-Edward Abbey, Desert Solitaire

People of the Past

How many ways can you use the word "pinto"? You probably know that it's a name for a spotted horse and a bean. But did you know that it's also a name for an ancient people of the Desert Southwest?

The Pinto people lived in small bands. They moved often, hunting game and gathering plants. The remains of one of their camps lie in Pinto Basin, near where a stream used to flow over 4,000 years ago.

That camp is a *type site* for the Pinto Culture. That means that if the same uniquely-shaped spear and knife points found in Pinto Basin are discovered at another *archaeological site*, the people who lived at that site are considered part of the same culture.

P is for the **Pinto Basin**,
Where ancient people used to walk.
What stories do you think you'd hear
If coyotes and cacti could talk?

P

Q is for **Quail Mountain**—
What just ran across the trail?
Topknots bobbing on their heads,
Must be mom and baby quail!

Q

R is for **Rock-climbing**.
There's some danger way up high.
But if you learn to do it safely,
It's a sport that's fun to try.

R

Slither Away

Can you find an "S" in the sand? That means a sidewinder, a horned rattlesnake, has just passed through, sideways, before you. But don't worry! Chances are slim it would ever bother you. It was probably looking for a place to hide and ambush a mouse for its next meal.

In the desert, snakes rule! They don't need lots of water, they like heat, and they can go days without eating. Even without legs, snakes are skilled hunters who eat rodents, insects, and even other snakes. They play an important role in the *ecosystem* by keeping down the numbers of small critters like mice and rats.

Though you might not actually see a snake in Joshua Tree, you may be lucky enough to see the ghost of one. Several times a year snakes shed their skin, leaving a thin, crinkly cast-off of their long, skinny shape.

The rosy boa found in the park is one of the few *constrictors* living in the desert. Constrictors coil themselves around prey and squeeze it to death.

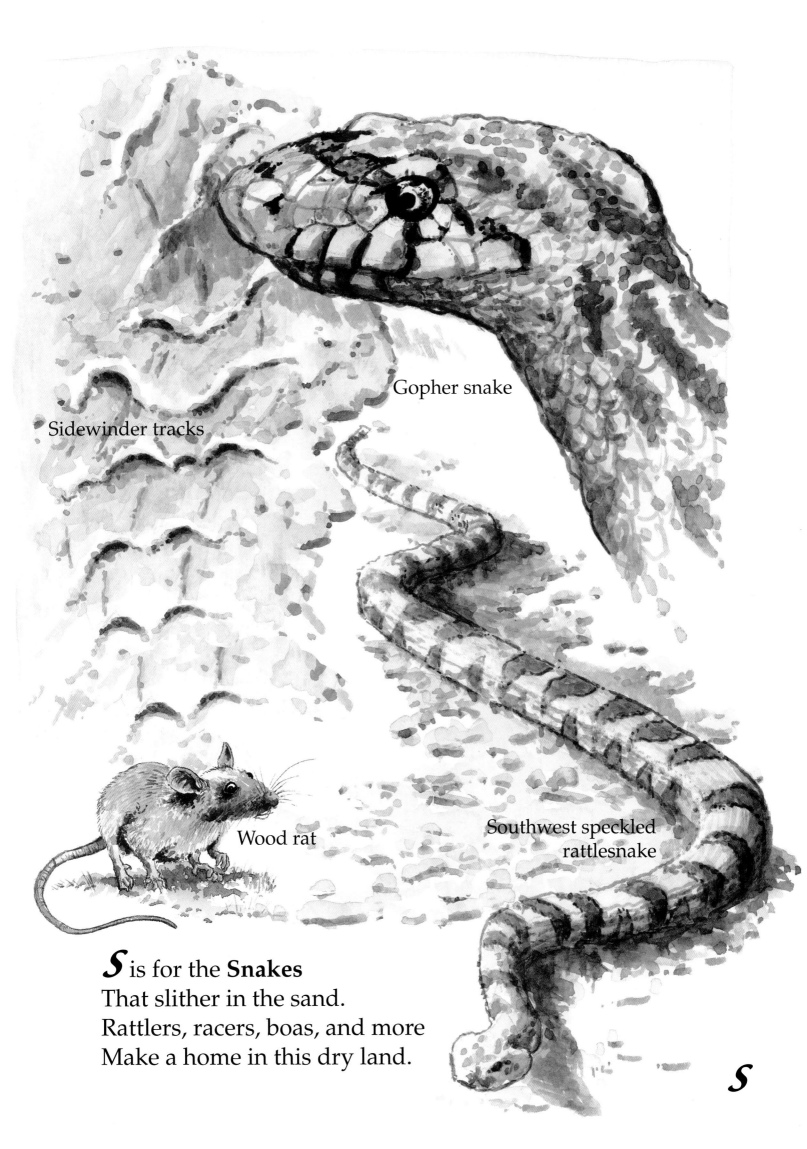

Sidewinder tracks

Gopher snake

Wood rat

Southwest speckled
rattlesnake

S is for the **Snakes**
That slither in the sand.
Rattlers, racers, boas, and more
Make a home in this dry land.

S

Threatened...

The desert tortoise has adapted to its harsh environment by living life in the slow lane. It spends the winter hibernating in burrows—which can be as long as 30 feet—and often passes hot summer days holed up in the sand as well. It comes out in the cool morning hours, or at night, to graze on shrubs.

Desert tortoises are a *threatened species*. Lots of them are killed by cars. Cattle and sheep ruin their *habitat*.

Life for a tortoise begins against the odds. After babies hatch, their mother doesn't care for them. The soft-shelled young are easy pickings for *predators* like coyotes. As few as 1 in over 100 survive. Those which do survive can live for over 100 years.

Tortoises are protected in the park and other reserves by not allowing grazing or off-road driving, and by limiting other activities that destroy their desert home.

T is for the **Desert Tortoise**,
Protected by its shell.
A species that is threatened, they're
Protected by the law as well.

T

U is for the **Uniforms**
In shades of green and gray
Worn by the park employees
Who will help you on your way.

u

U Can Be One!

Joshua Tree is a place where plants and animals have developed cool survival strategies. Once you understand some of these *adaptations*, you will never see the desert in the same way. You'll have a new respect for everything that lives in this harsh, dry land.

A good way to learn more about the park is to become a Junior Ranger. You can pick up a Junior Ranger workbook at any entrance station or visitor center. Activities include drawing, attending ranger programs, playing games, looking for animal tracks, and picking up litter.

Once you finish several activities, a ranger will review your workbook, sign it, and award you a Junior Ranger badge. You can be proud of that badge! It means you're helping to keep the park a special place, and having fun while you're at it.

Very Efficient Recycling

Do you think recycling is a new idea? If so, you're partly right. People only recently started recycling their waste. But recycling has been going on in the natural world for as long as there's been a natural world.

Whenever an animal dies, its body becomes food for *scavengers* like vultures, coyotes, and ravens. Tiny *organisms* like insects, bacteria, and *fungi* complete the process of recycling the dead. They are called *decomposers*, creatures that eat waste and return its energy to the earth.

Dead plants are also recycled. A dead Joshua tree, for example, not only provides homes for all kinds of critters, but also food for decomposers. They might take years to eat such a big plant, but eventually only dust will remain.

Earth's recycling process starts with the sun, which is the source of all the planet's energy. Plants use sunlight, water, and minerals from the soil to make their food. Then animals eat the plants. Animal waste becomes soil, which other plants use for food. Round and round it goes...

Nature wastes nothing. Is that a lesson for us?

V is for the **Vultures**
Gliding at a dizzy height,
Searching for dead animals
By smell as well as sight.

Wild, Wild, Wildflowers

After a long dry spell, it rains in the desert. In a matter of days, wildflowers carpet the land, and once-brown valleys burst with color.

The beauty of its flowering plants, especially cacti, attracted tourists to the southern California desert. Unfortunately, many people wanted to take some of that beauty home with them. But if everyone took even just one plant home, there'd be little left for the rest of us to see.

So, during the 1920s, a Los Angeles woman named Minerva Holt led efforts to protect the area. President Franklin Roosevelt set aside 825,000 acres as Joshua Tree National Monument in 1936. The monument became a national park in 1994. Its wildflowers will now stay in the wild for all to enjoy.

Spindly sticks afire! Bright dashes of orange bring the ocotillo to life in springtime bloom. Look closely! Maybe a hummingbird will come for a sip of its nectar.

Beavertail cactus

Desert monkeyflower

Prickly pear
cactus

Canterbury
bells

W is for **Wildflowers**,
A carpet of color after a rain—
A beautiful, wonderful, dazzling sight
That draws people back here again and again.

w

X Marks the SPOT!

Oasis Visitor Center

Eagle Mountains
see page E

Quail Mountain
see page Q

Indian Cove
see page I

Keys Ranch
see page K

Visitor Center

Oasis (1 of 5)
see page O

Cottonwo
Visitor Ce

Pinto Basin
see page P

Joshua Tree, in southeastern
California, was proclaimed a
National Monument in 1936.
It became a National Park in 1994.

Xtra FUN things to DO and SEE

Mojave Desert

Colorado Desert

Rock Climb
Scramble up a rock formation in the Wilderness of Rocks. But be careful! Don't climb too high. Have someone "spot" you (stand beneath you) to catch you if you slip. And remember...it's a lot easier to get up than it is to get down!

Hike
Take a short walk to Barker Dam, built in the 1930s to store water for cattle. This rain-fed reservoir is a great place to look for bighorn sheep and other wildlife.

Time Travel
Visit the Desert Queen Ranch to see how kids lived years ago in this isolated desert. You can see an orchard, a dam, a schoolhouse, and some of the machinery that Bill Keys built from scrap and junk.

X marks the spot
Where you can make your mark
Of all the places you explored
In Joshua Tree National Park.

X

Yucca: One-Stop Shopping

Before there were grocery stores, the Indians who lived around here relied on desert plants and animals for all their food, clothing, and medicine.

Yucca had many uses. Its flowers were eaten raw, or boiled. Seeds were dried, then ground into a flour that could be stored and eaten during the lean months of winter.

Yucca leaves were woven into sandals and baskets. The sharp tip of a leaf could be broken off, then pulled away from the plant with a few fibers attached to be used as a needle and thread. Yucca roots were pounded with rocks to make soap and shampoo.

Early desert people used every part of the yucca…on every part of their bodies from the tops of their heads to the bottoms of their feet.

Y is for the **Yucca Plant**.
Its flowers made a tasty treat,
Its roots were pounded into soap,
Its leaves made sandals for the feet.

Zillions of Things We Missed

There's way more to do and see in the park than would fit in this book. Stop at a visitor center to get all the information you need to plan a great visit.

☆ Millions of years of earth history are on display along Geology Tour Road, one of the park's weirdest, wildest rockscapes.

☆ There are over 250 documented *archaeological sites* in the park, with rock art, *middens, potsherds, grinding holes,* and more. Please remember: disturbing a site or removing *artifacts* destroys valuable scientific information and is against the law.

☆ The stars come out at night! Nine campgrounds in the park offer a chance to enjoy the beauty of the night sky.

And don't forget the small stuff: like tiny flowers blooming in the cracks of rocks, and a zillion other discoveries awaiting young adventurers who take the time to look, listen, and learn.

Costa's hummingbird

Pronuba moth
see page 47

Coyote

Skull Rock

Elephant Rock

Seal Rock

Z is for **Zooming in**
On all the things we missed.
The stuff that you can see and do
Makes far too long a list.

Z

What do you mean by . . . ?

adaptation (ad´əp tā´shən)—a change made by a species of plant or animal that makes it better suited to survive in a particular environment

archaeological site (är´kē ə loj´i kəl sīt)—a place that contains physical evidence of past human activity

artifact (är´tə fakt´)—something made by humans

diversity (di vûr´si tē)—the number and different kinds of animals, plants, and other organisms in a place

ecosystem (ek´ ō sis´təm)—a community of plants and animals, the environment they live in, and everything that happens among them

endangered species (en dān´jərd spē´shēz)—a species in danger of becoming *extinct*

extinct (ik stiṉgkt)—no longer existing

fungi (fun´jī)—a group of organisms that eat organic matter and don't use sunlight to make food like plants do

grinding hole (grīndiṉg hōl)—a smooth bowl in a rock made by grinding grain or seeds with another rock

habitat (hab´i tat´)—the place where an animal or plant lives

midden (mid´ən)—a pile or layer of trash left by the humans who lived in a place

oasis (ōā´sis)—a fertile spot in the midst of a desert created by the presence of water

organism (ôr´gə niz´əm)—any living thing

potsherd (pot´shûrd´)—a piece of broken pottery

predator (pred´ə tər)—an animal that kills and eats other animals

scavenger (skav´in jər)—an animal that eats bodies of animals abandoned by *predators*, scrounges through garbage, eats roadkill, etc.; many animals such as coyotes aren't just scavengers, but also kill live prey

stamp mill (stamp mil)—a contraption with big steel rods (called stamps) that crush ore to separate the metal from the rock

teamster (tēm´stər)—when first used, this word meant someone who hauled freight with a wagon; now it also means someone who drives trucks for a living

threatened species (thret´ənd spē´shēz)—a species likely to become *endangered*

type site (tīp sīt)—an *archaeological site* that contains artifacts such as spear points or pottery that are used to define and name a culture

Did you know that . . . ?

. . .The Joshua tree would cease to exist if not for the pronuba moth. The female moth lays her eggs in the trees' flowers, spreading pollen in the process. The flowers can only make seeds after they have been dusted with pollen from another flower.

. . .A Joshua tree completely burned in a fire probably won't die, but will survive in the form of a sprout that emerges from the tree's unburned roots.

. . .There are no year-round free-flowing streams or other natural bodies of water anywhere in the park.

Leave No Trace©!

Leave No Trace! is just another way to say . . . leave the park the same or better than you found it. Pack out your trash, and pick up somebody else's, too! Leave all rocks, flowers, *artifacts*, antlers, and bones in their place exactly as you found them. Then others can enjoy the beauty of Joshua Tree National Park just like you.

More books you'll enjoy!

101 Questions About Desert Life, by ALICE JABLONSKY. Southwest Parks and Monuments Association.
America's Deserts: Guide to Plants and Animals, by MARIANNE D. WALLACE. Fulcrum Kids Publishing.
The Cactus Coloring Book, by STEFEN BERNATH & CAROLYN S. RIPPS. Dover Publications, Inc.
Creatures of the Desert World, illustrated by BARBARA GIBSON. A National Geographic Action Book.
Joshua Tree: The Story Behind the Scenery, by DELCIE H. VUNCANNON. KC Publications.
Southwest Desert Animals: A Pictorial Guide & Identification of Wild Animals of our Southwest, by BENNETT WILSON. Plateau Productions.

What Does the Future Hold?

The desert is home to an amazing cast of plants and animals, and an increasing number of humans. Yet it takes special adaptations to live in a land of little water and baking sun. Will those who live next door to the park be willing to adapt like the plants and animals have?

Water is scarce in the desert. Electricity is expensive and not always reliable. It takes careful planning to maintain things people want—from swimming pools to air conditioning—in a warm desert home.

If the park's neighbors conserve water and wildlife habitat by landscaping with native plants, build energy-efficient homes, and use solar and wind power, it will help keep Joshua Tree National Park a special place. Remember: how we act outside the park affects life inside the park.

For more information about Joshua Tree National Park, visit **www.nps.gov/jotr**

KC Publications has been the leading publisher of colorful, interpretive books about National Park areas, public lands, Indian lands, and related subjects for over 38 years. We have 6 active series—over 125 titles—with Translation Packages in up to 8 languages for over half the areas we cover. Write, call, or visit our web site for our full-color catalog.

Our series are:

The Story Behind the Scenery® – Compelling stories of over 65 National Park areas and similar Public Land areas. Some with Translation Packages.

in pictures... The Continuing Story® – A companion, pictorially oriented, series on America's National Parks. All titles have Translation Packages.

For Young Adventurers™ – Dedicated to young seekers and keepers of all things wild and sacred. Explore America's Heritage from A to Z.

Voyage of Discovery™ – Exploration of the expansion of the western United States.

Indian Culture and the Southwest – All about Native Americans, past and present.

Calendars – For National Parks and Southwest Indian culture, in dramatic full color, and a companion Color Your Own series, with crayons.

To receive our full-color catalog featuring over 125 titles—Books, Calendars, Screen Scenes, Videos, Audio Tapes, and other related specialty products:

Call (800-626-9673), fax (702-433-3420), write to the address below, Or visit our web site at www.kcpublications.com

Published by KC Publications, 3245 E. Patrick Ln., Suite A, Las Vegas, NV 89120.

Inside back cover:
Day is done.

Back cover:
Like young adventurers everywhere, this coyote pup needs his rest.

Created, Designed, and Published in the U.S.A.
Printed by Tien Wah Press (Pte.) Ltd, Singapore
Color Separations by United Graphic Pte. Ltd